DI
ON TI
—

*By*

CHARLES DICKENS

WITH AN
INTRODUCTION BY
F. G. KITTON

# CONTENTS

# INTRODUCTION

By F. G. Kitton

## Political Squibs from
## *The Examiner*, 1841

In August 1841 Dickens contributed anonymously to *The Examiner* (then edited by Forster) three political squibs, which were signed W., and were intended to help the Liberals in fighting their opponents. These squibs were entitled respectively *The Fine Old English Gentleman (to be said or sung at all Conservative Dinners)*; *The Quack Doctor's Proclamation*; and *Subjects for Painters (after Peter Pindar)*. Concerning those productions, Forster says: 'I doubt if he ever enjoyed anything more than the power of thus taking part occasionally, unknown to outsiders, in the sharp conflict the press was waging at the time.' In all probability he contributed other political rhymes to the pages of *The Examiner* as events prompted: if so, they are buried beyond easy reach of identification.

Writing to Forster at this time, Dickens said: 'By Jove, how Radical I am getting! I wax stronger and stronger in the true principles every day '. . . He would (observes Forster) sometimes even talk, in moments of sudden indignation at the political outlook, 'of carrying off himself and his household gods, like Coriolanus, to a world elsewhere.' This was the period of the Tory interregnum, with Sir Robert Peel at the head of affairs.

## Verses from the
*Daily News,* 1846

The *Daily News*, it will be remembered, was founded in January 1846 by Charles Dickens, who officiated as its first editor. He soon sickened of the mechanical drudgery appertaining to the position, and resigned his editorial functions the following month. From January 21st to March 2nd he contributed to its columns a series of 'Travelling Sketches,' afterwards reprinted in volume form as *Pictures from Italy.* He also availed himself of the opportunity afforded him, by his association with that newspaper, of once more taking up the cudgels against the Tories, and, as in the case of the *Examiner*, his attack was conveyed through the medium of some doggerel verses. These were entitled *The British Lion—A New Song, but an Old Story, to be sung to the tune of 'The Great Sea-Snake.* They bore the signature of 'Catnach,' the famous ballad-singer, and were printed in the *Daily News* of January 24, 1846.

Three weeks later some verses of a totally different character appeared in the columns of the *Daily News*, signed in full 'CHARLES DICKENS'.

One Lucy Simpkins, of Bremhill (or Bremble), a parish in Wiltshire, had just previously addressed a night meeting of the wives of agricultural labourers in that county, in support of a petition for Free Trade, and her vigorous speech on that occasion inspired Dickens to write *The Hymn of the Wiltshire Labourers*, thus offering an earnest protest against oppression. Concerning the 'Hymn,' a writer in a recent issue of *Christmas Bells* observes: 'It breathes in every line the teaching of the Sermon on the Mount, the love of the All-Father, the Redemption by His Son, and that love to God and man on which hang all the law and the prophets.'

EXCERPTS FROM
*The Poems and Verses of Charles Dickens*, 1903

# THE FINE OLD
# ENGLISH GENTLEMAN

---

*To be Said or Sung at All Conservative Dinners*

I'll sing you a new ballad, and I'll warrant it first-rate,
Of the days of that old gentleman who had that old estate;
When they spent the public money at a bountiful old rate
On ev'ry mistress, pimp, and scamp, at ev'ry noble gate,
   In the fine old English Tory times;
   Soon may they come again!

The good old laws were garnished well with gibbets, whips,
 and chains,
With fine old English penalties, and fine old English pains,
With rebel heads, and seas of blood once hot in rebel veins;
For all these things were requisite to guard the rich old gains
   Of the fine old English Tory times;
   Soon may they come again!

This brave old code, like Argus, had a hundred watchful eyes,
And ev'ry English peasant had his good old English spies,
To tempt his starving discontent with fine old English lies,
Then call the good old Yeomanry to stop his peevish cries,
        In the fine old English Tory times;
        Soon may they come again!

The good old times for cutting throats that cried out in their need,
The good old times for hunting men who held their fathers' creed,
The good old times when William Pitt, as all good men agreed,
Came down direct from Paradise at more than railroad speed...
        Oh the fine old English Tory times;
        When will they come again!

In those rare days, the press was seldom known to snarl or bark,
But sweetly sang of men in pow'r, like any tuneful lark;
Grave judges, too, to all their evil deeds were in the dark;
And not a man in twenty score knew how to make his mark.
        Oh the fine old English Tory times;
        Soon may they come again!

Those were the days for taxes, and for war's infernal din;
For scarcity of bread, that fine old dowagers might win;
For shutting men of letters up, through iron bars to grin,
Because they didn't think the Prince was altogether thin,

         In the fine old English Tory times;
         Soon may they come again!


But Tolerance, though slow in flight, is strong-wing'd
   in the main;
That night must come on these fine days, in course of time
   was plain;
The pure old spirit struggled, but its struggles were in vain;
A nation's grip was on it, and it died in choking pain,

         With the fine old English Tory days,
         All of the olden time.


The bright old day now dawns again; the cry runs through
   the land,
In England there shall be dear bread—in Ireland, sword
   and brand;
And poverty, and ignorance, shall swell the rich and grand,
So, rally round the rulers with the gentle iron hand,

         Of the fine old English Tory days;
         Hail to the coming time!

# THE
# QUACK DOCTOR'S
# PROCLAMATION

---

TO THE TUNE

*A Cobbler There Was*


An astonishing doctor has just come to town,
Who will do all the faculty perfectly brown:
He knows all diseases, their causes, and ends;
And he begs to appeal to his medical friends.

> Tol de rol:
> Diddle doll:
> Tol de rol, de dol,
> Diddle doll
> Tol de rol doll.


He's a magnetic doctor, and knows how to keep
The whole of a Government snoring asleep
To popular clamours; till popular pins
Are stuck in their midriffs—and then he begins

> Tol de rol.

He's a *clairvoyant* subject, and readily reads
His countrymen's wishes, condition, and needs,
With many more fine things I can't tell in rhyme,
—And he keeps both his eyes shut the whole of the time.

> Tol de rol.

You mustn't expect him to talk; but you'll take
Most particular notice the doctor's awake,
Though for aught from his words or his looks that you reap, he
Might just as well be most confoundedly sleepy.

> Tol de rol.

Homœopathy, too, he has practised for ages
(You'll find his prescriptions in Luke Hansard's pages),
Just giving his patient when maddened by pain,—
Of Reform the ten thousandth part of a grain.

> Tol de rol.

He's a med'cine for Ireland, in portable papers;
The infallible cure for political vapours;
A neat label round it his 'prentices tie—
'Put your trust in the Lord, and keep this powder dry!'

> Tol de rol.

He's a corn doctor also, of wonderful skill,
—No cutting, no rooting-up, purging, or pill—
You're merely to take, 'stead of walking or riding,
The sweet schoolboy exercise—innocent sliding.

> Tol de rol.

There's no advice gratis. If high ladies send
His legitimate fee, he's their soft-spoken friend.
At the great public counter with one hand behind him,
And one in his waistcoat, they're certain to find him.

> Tol de rol.

He has only to add he's the real Doctor Flam,
All others being purely fictitious and sham;
The house is a large one, tall, slated, and white,
With a lobby; and lights in the passage at night.

> Tol de rol:
> Diddle doll:
> Tol de rol, de dol,
> Diddle doll
> Tol de rol doll.

# SUBJECTS
# FOR PAINTERS

———

*After Peter Pindar*

To you, Sir Martin, and your co. R.A.'s,
I dedicate in meek, suggestive lays,
Some subjects for your academic palettes;
Hoping, by dint of these my scanty jobs,
To fill with novel thoughts your teeming nobs,
As though I beat them in with wooden mallets.

To you, Maclise, who Eve's fair daughters paint
With Nature's hand, and want the maudlin taint
Of the sweet Chalon school of silk and ermine:
To you, E. Landseer, who from year to year
Delight in beasts and birds, and dogs and deer,
And seldom give us any human vermin:
—To all who practise art, or make believe,
I offer subjects they may take or leave.

Great Sibthorp and his butler, in debate
        (*Arcades ambo*) on affairs of state,
Not altogether 'gone,' but rather funny;
        Cursing the Whigs for leaving in the lurch
        Our d—d good, pleasant, gentlemanly Church,
Would make a picture—cheap at any money.


Or Sibthorp as the Tory Sec.—at-War,
        Encouraging his mates with loud 'Yhor! Yhor!
From Treas'ry benches' most conspicuous end;
        Or Sib.'s mustachios curling with a smile,
        As an expectant Premier without guile
Calls him his honourable and gallant friend.


Or Sibthorp travelling in foreign parts,
        Through that rich portion of our Eastern charts
Where lies the land of popular tradition;
        And fairly worshipp'd by the true devout
        In all his comings-in and goings-out,
Because of the old Turkish superstition.

Fame with her trumpet, blowing very hard,
    And making earth rich with celestial lard,
In puffing deeds done through Lord Chamberlain Howe;
    While some few thousand persons of small gains,
    Who give their charities without such pains,
Look up, much wondering what may be the row.


Behind them Joseph Hume, who turns his pate
    To where great Marlbro' House in princely state
Shelters a host of lacqueys, lords and pages,
    And says he knows of dowagers a crowd,
    Who, without trumpeting so very loud,
Would do so much, and more, for half the wages.


Limn, sirs, the highest lady in the land,
    When Joseph Surface, fawning cap in hand,
Delivers in his list of patriot mortals;
    Those gentlemen of honour, faith, and truth,
    Who, foul-mouthed, spat upon her maiden youth,
And dog-like did defile her palace portals.

Paint me the Tories, full of grief and woe,
Weeping (to voters) over Frost and Co.,
Their suff'ring, erring, much-enduring brothers.
And in the background don't forget to pack,
Each grinning ghastly from its bloody sack,
The heads of Thistlewood, Despard, and others.

Paint, squandering the club's election gold,
Fierce lovers of our Constitution old,
Lords who're that sacred lady's greatest debtors;
And let the law, forbidding any voice
Or act of Peer to influence the choice
Of English people, flourish in bright letters.

Paint that same dear old lady, ill at ease,
Weak in her second childhood, hard to please,
Unknowing what she ails or what she wishes;
With all her Carlton nephews at the door,
Deaf'ning both aunt and nurses with their roar,
—Fighting already, for the loaves and fishes.

Leaving these hints for you to dwell upon,
I shall presume to offer more anon.

# THE
# BRITISH LION
# A NEW SONG,
# BUT AN OLD STORY

TO THE TUNE
*The Great Sea-Snake*

Oh, p'r'aps you may have heard, and if not, I'll sing
    Of the British Lion free,
That was constantly a-going for to make a spring
    Upon his en-e-me;
But who, being rather groggy at the knees,
    Broke down, always, before;
And generally gave a feeble wheeze
    Instead of a loud roar.
        Right toor rol, loor rol, fee faw fum,
           The British Lion bold!
        That was always a-going for to do great things,
           And was always being 'sold!'

He was carried about, in a carawan,
 And was show'd in country parts,
And they said, 'Walk up! Be in time! He can
 Eat Corn-Law Leagues like tarts!'
And his showmen, shouting there and then,
 To puff him didn't fail,
And they said, as they peep'd into his den,
 'Oh, don't he wag his tail!'


Now, the principal keeper of this poor old beast,
 WAN HUMBUG was his name,
Would once ev'ry day stir him up—at least—
 And wasn't that a Game!
For he hadn't a tooth, and he hadn't a claw,
 In that 'Struggle' so 'Sublime';
And, however sharp they touch'd him on the raw,
 He couldn't come up to time.

And this, you will observe, was the reason why
    WAN HUMBUG, on weak grounds,
Was forced to make believe that he heard his cry
    In all unlikely sounds.
So, there wasn't a bleat from an Essex Calf,
    Or a Duke, or a Lordling slim;
But he said, with a wery triumphant laugh,
    'I'm blest if that ain't him.'


At length, wery bald in his mane and tail,
    The British Lion growed:
He pined, and declined, and he satisfied
    The last debt which he owed.
And when they came to examine the skin,
    It was a wonder sore,
To find that the an-i-mal within
    Was nothing but a Boar!
        Right toor rol, loor rol, fee faw fum,
            The British Lion bold!
        That was always a-going for to do great things,
            And was always being 'sold!'

# THE HYMN
# OF THE
# WILTSHIRE LABOURERS

—————

'Don't you all think that we have a great need to Cry to
our God to put it in the hearts of our greassous Queen
and her Members of Parlerment to grant us free bread!'
— LUCY SIMPKINS

Oh God, who by Thy Prophet's hand
    Didst smite the rocky brake,
Whence water came, at Thy command,
    Thy people's thirst to slake;
Strike, now, upon this granite wall,
    Stern, obdurate, and high;
And let some drops of pity fall
    For us who starve and die!

The God, who took a little child,
   And set him in the midst,
And promised him His mercy mild,
   As, by Thy Son, Thou didst:
Look down upon our children dear,
   So gaunt, so cold, so spare,
And let their images appear
   Where Lords and Gentry are!

Oh God, teach them to feel how we,
   When our poor infants droop,
Are weakened in our trust in Thee,
   And how our spirits stoop;
For, in Thy rest, so bright and fair,
   All tears and sorrows sleep:
And their young looks, so full of care,
   Would make Thine Angels weep!

The God, who with His finger drew
    The Judgment coming on,
Write, for these men, what must ensue,
    Ere many years be gone!
Oh God, whose bow is in the sky,
    Let them not brave and dare,
Until they look (too late) on high,
    And see an Arrow there!


Oh God, remind them! In the bread
    They break upon the knee,
These sacred words may yet be read,
    'In memory of Me!'
Oh God, remind them of His sweet
    Compassion for the poor,
And how He gave them Bread to eat,
    And went from door to door!

Printed in Great Britain
by Amazon

62349961R00017